CONTENTS

Words in **bold** can be found in the glossary on page 28

Shaping materials

Everything around you is made up of materials. Everyday materials include paper, plastic, metal and glass. We use these materials to make objects such as tables and chairs, shoes, clothes, cars and aircraft.

↓ *All these objects are plastic. They were made by putting liquid plastic into* **moulds.**

Shaping
Materials

Chris Oxlade

WAYLAND

First published in Great Britain in 2006 by Wayland,
an imprint of Hachette Children's Books

Copyright © 2006 Wayland

Hachette Children's Books
338 Euston Road, London NW1 3BH

Editor: Hayley Leach
Senior Design Manager: Rosamund Saunders
Designer: Ben Ruocco
Photographer: Philip Wilkins

British Library Cataloguing in Publication Data
Oxlade, Chris
  Shaping materials. - (Working with materials)
  1.Machining - Juvenile literature
  I.Title
  671.3'5

ISBN-10: 0-7502-4902-1
ISBN-13: 978-0-7502-4902-7

Cover photograph: a potter is using clay to make a pot.
Photo credits: 1Apix/Alamy 6, Ute Kaiser/zefa/Corbis 7,
Richard Jung/Photolibrary.com 8, Michael Keller/Corbis 9,
Jeremy Liebman/Getty Images 10, Jeff Morgan/Alamy 11,
Fortune fish/Alamy 12, Paul Jones/Getty Images 13,
Chris Oxlade 14, Xela/Alamy 15, Darrin Jenkins/Alamy 16,
Chris Alack/Getty Images 17, Steve Allen/Science Photo Library 18,
Joel Sartore/National Geographic/Getty Images 19,
Tom Stewart/Corbis cover and 20, Janine Wiedel Photolibrary
/Alamy 21, Rosenfield Images Ltd/Science Photo Library 22,
Tim Caddick/Alamy 23, Peter Weimann/Photolibrary.com 24,
R. Maisonneuve, Publiphoto Diffusion/Science Photo Library 25,
Philip Wilkins 26-27.

The publishers would like to thank the models Philippa and Sophie
Campbell for appearing in the photographs.

← *A dress-maker is cutting a piece of fabric into the shape she wants using a pair of scissors.*

Some materials come in blocks or sheets. Others come as liquids or powders. Cutting, folding and moulding are some ways of shaping materials into objects. The method we use depends on the **properties** of the material.

Scissors and saws

Cutting with scissors is a simple way of making shapes from materials such as paper, card and fabric. A pair of scissors has two sharp blades that slice through the material.

↓ *This cook is cutting pastry shapes. The pastry cutter has a sharp metal blade.*

← A **carpenter** cutting
a piece of wood with
a saw to make the
shape he wants.

It's a Fact!

When saw blades are
made, they are heated
and then dipped in
water. This makes
them extra hard.

We cut through thick pieces of material,
such as wood, with a saw. A saw
blade has hundreds of sharp grooves
called teeth. As the saw moves
backwards and forwards, the teeth rip
away tiny bits of material.

Carving materials

An artist can make a wooden sculpture by carving a block of wood. The artist cuts bits off the block using a knife, or a sharp tool called a chisel. It takes lots of skill to cut away the right bits.

↓ *An artist shaping wood with a chisel.*

↑ *A stone mason chips away stone with a hammer and chisel.*

Artists, called stone masons, work with stone. They start with a block of stone and gradually chip away pieces to make the shape they want. We also shape stone blocks to make the walls of buildings.

It's a Fact!

The Ancient Egyptians built giant stone pyramids using thousands of stone blocks. Workers cut the blocks using simple hand tools.

Folding and bending

We can make objects by folding
and bending flat sheets of material.
For example, we make envelopes
and paper bags by folding paper.
Cardboard boxes are made by
folding stiff cardboard.

← *You can make
shapes, such as this
flower, by folding a
piece of paper.*

↑ *This tent has metal poles. The poles are bent over to make the dome shape of the tent.*

Bending lets us make rounded shapes from flat sheets of materials. For example, shoes are made by bending leather around a wooden block called a last.

It's a Fact!

A curved wooden chair seat is made by bending flat sheets of wood. The wood is heated with steam to make it easier to bend.

Machine shapers

Many objects are shaped by machines. The machines have blades that cut away material from a block. This leaves the shape that is wanted.

← This machine cuts wood into shape. The blade in the middle spins to cut away the wood.

↑ *A carpenter making an*
  ornament on a lathe.

Carpenters and metalworkers often
use a machine called a lathe.
It makes round objects, such as rods
and poles. The material spins round
at high speed. A blade cuts away
the material.

It's a Fact!

Computers control
machines to make
objects like nuts and
bolts. The computer
automatically moves the
material and the blades
to cut the shape.

Moulding materials

Chocolates, ice cubes and washing-up bowls all have something in common. They are all made in a mould.
A mould has a **hollow** space inside. The hollow space is the shape of the object being made.

↓ *Chocolate is warmed up to make it soft. Then it is poured into moulds. It goes hard again when it cools down.*

← *Jellies are made by putting a warm jelly mixture into a mould. The jelly turns solid when it cools.*

Runny material is poured into the mould. It fills the mould to make a new object. The runny material gradually goes hard. Then the object is taken out of the mould. Now the mould is ready to be used again.

Moulding in industry

Nearly all plastic things are made by moulding. The plastic is warmed up to make it soft. Then it is put into a mould. When the plastic cools the object is taken out of the mould. Glass objects are also made in moulds.

↓ *This plastic bin has just been taken out of its mould.*

↑ *This is molten copper. It is being poured into a mould.*

Some metal objects are made in moulds. The metal is heated up until it melts. The **molten** metal is poured into a mould. When the metal cools down it turns solid again.

It's a Fact!

Builders use moulds to make concrete shapes. They build wooden moulds and then pour concrete in. When the concrete is hard, they take away the wood.

Shaping soft materials

Some materials are easy to shape when they are very soft. Potter's clay is very soft. You can easily shape it with your hands. A potter uses simple tools to shape clay.

← *This potter is using her hands to shape a clay pot.*

↑ *This glassblower is making a glass vase by blowing air into a blob of hot, soft glass.*

Glass is normally very hard and it can break easily. Glass goes soft when it is heated. Glassblowers shape glass when it is hot with special tools. Then they let the glass cool and go hard.

It's a Fact!

Soft materials, like cake icing, can be pushed through a small hole. This makes a long, thin piece of material.

Shaping metals

Iron, steel, **aluminium** and copper are all types of metal. They are strong and hard. We shape metals by cutting them and by moulding them.

↓ *This machine is cutting a sheet of metal using a **laser**.*

← *This machine is pressing a metal object into shape.*

It's a Fact!

The round shape of a coin is cut from a sheet of metal. Then another machine presses the picture onto each side of the coin.

We can squash, stretch, bend and twist a piece of metal. We make objects such as metal bowls and tin lids by pressing sheets of metal into shape.

Hammering and rolling metals

A blacksmith makes things, such as **horseshoes** and garden gates, from iron. The blacksmith heats up the iron. This makes the iron softer and easier for the blacksmith to hammer into shape.

↓ *A blacksmith making a horseshoe. He is working on a heavy block of iron called an anvil.*

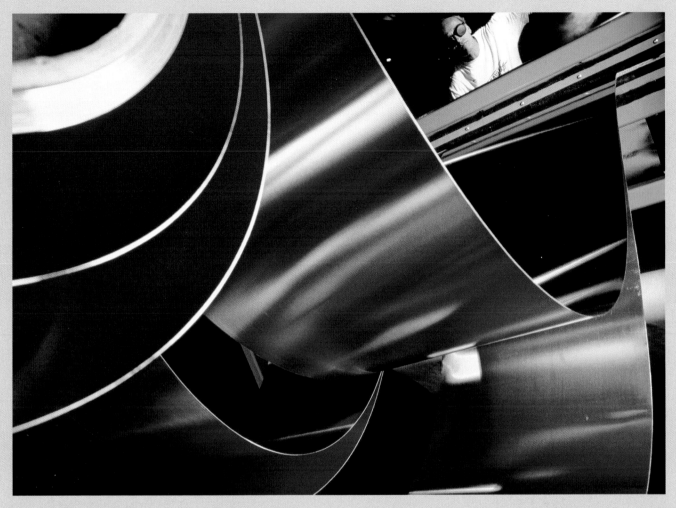

↑ *Copper is rolled into sheets.*

Thin sheets of metal, such as steel, are made by rollers. The metal starts as a block. The metal is heated up to make it easier to roll. It goes through many rollers. It gradually gets thinner and thinner.

It's a Fact!

Metal wire is used to make things like paper clips. Wire is made by stretching a piece of metal a bit at a time. The metal gets thinner and longer.

25

Activities

Moulding ice shapes

Create your own mould so you can make different ice shapes.

What you need	
modelling clay	water
plastic food wrap	small object (such as a
old saucer	toy building block)

(1) Flatten a large lump of modelling clay until it is about 2 cm thick and about 8 cm across.

(2) Lay a piece of plastic food wrap loosely over the top of the modelling clay.

(3) Press an object firmly into the top of the modelling clay. Now take it off again. You have made a mould of the object.

(4) Put the mould on a saucer. Carefully fill the mould with water.

(5) Put the saucer in the freezer.

(6) When frozen, carefully take the ice out of the mould. You have made a copy of the object out of ice.

Making a box

Find out how to make a box by cutting and folding.

What you need	
pencil	scissors
ruler	sticky tape
card	

① Copy the pattern here onto a piece
   of card. Cut along the solid lines.
   Do not cut along the dotted lines.

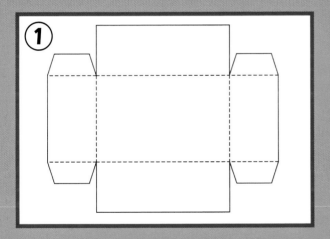

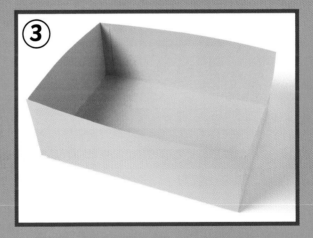

② Bend the card along all the dotted
   lines. Fold all the side panels up and
   then fold the end tabs around.

③ Using sticky tape, fix the end tabs to
   the side panels. You have made a box.

Glossary

aluminium a type of metal which is strong but lightweight

carpenter a person who makes things from wood

horseshoe a curved piece of iron nailed to a horse's foot

hollow an empty space inside a mould

laser a device that makes a beam of light

molten when something is heated until it melts

mould to make an object into a mould

runny when something flows like a liquid, such as water

property tells us what a material is like. The hardness of a material and how easily it melts are examples of properties.

Further information

BOOKS

How We Use: Metals/Paper/Rubber/Wood
by Chris Oxlade, Raintree (2005)

A Material World: It's Glass/It's Metal/It's Plastic/It's Wood
by Kay Davies and Wendy Oldfield, Wayland (2006)

Investigating Science: How do we use materials?
by Jacqui Bailey, Franklin Watts (2005)

WEBSITES

www.bbc.co.uk/schools/revisewise/science/materials/09_act.shtml
Animated examples and quiz about changing materials

www.strangematterexhibit.com
Fun site about the properties of materials

PLACES TO VISIT

Eureka, Halifax
www.eureka.org.uk

Glasgow Science Centre
www.glasgowsciencecentre.org

The Science Museum, London
www.sciencemuseum.org.uk

29

Index

All the numbers in **bold**
refer to photographs